The Ombudsman of a New World Order

*Speech &
Sermons on
World Peace &
World
Governments*

Emmanuel Adetula

Copyright © 2011 by Emmanuel Adetula.

ISBN: Softcover 0-9798136-3-8

This book was printed in the United States of America.

To order additional copies of this book, Contact:
Emmanuel Adetula (Author)
P.o. Box 111589, Los Angeles, CA.90011, USA.
www.emmanueltula.com www.christchannelnetwork.com

Available in Book and DVD Video Format

Receive the complete package of this book and the DVD Video format shipped to you free with your donation to CCN Center for Religious Peace and New World Order.

Mail your donation to:- PO Box 111589, Los Angeles, CA 90011, USA.

www.emmanueltula.com.   www.christchannelnetwork.com

Contents

Note from the Author

CCN Center for Religious Peace and New World Order is an organization whose mission is to seek and pursue good governments, religious peace, liberty, and social justice. The organization promotes the rule of law, transitional justice, and democracy and features interviews and dialogues with political and religious leaders, as well as the academic community. The result of these dialogues and interviews produced excellent cross-cultural ideas and statements across the board, which then resulted in statements and speech and sermons that are not directly the creation of the author as produced in this book. Therefore, it should be noted by the readers that the book contains a lot of lifted matters not in the correct format (e.g., use of double quotation marks, citation of sources) for quoted materials. The quotations are not the accurate reproductions of the original. Therefore, it may appear to be with inconsistencies in interpolations since it did not carry the wording, spelling, capitalization, and internal punctuation of the original but is used by the author in his works to interpret the events of the time through his own messages, statements, and sermons as it appears in this book, *The Ombudsman of a New World Order*.

Religious Leaders and

the United States of America

in the Making of a New World Order

Socrates got into fatal trouble that led to the judges' verdict of the choice of death or banishment. Banishment in those days was the civic equivalent of death, and what was Socrates's sin? It was his declaration that he was not an Athenian or a Greek but "a citizen of the world." Two hundred years later, his works and writings for which he was found guilty ethos the formation of United Nations.

I am a man of strong ideas and opinion. What is unique about my opinions and ideas is that I always back them up with facts about what is going on in my own life and the lives of other human beings in other parts of the world, and this is what: put anything I say here to you under the classification of intellectual philosophical statements from a well-informed individual. So what you are about to hear from me are words from someone who has done his homework, which no doubt will put my critics in a very delicate position.

My critics cannot say that what I am about to tell you is not the truth. Anybody who is interested in the subject of the new world order that is in the making in our world today toward a one-world government can always look my statements up, and I don't waste my time arguing with people who are lazy to research the truth. Somebody may hate me for my strong opinions or big ideas or revolutionary, radical propositions or where I stand on issues or for taking it upon myself to be a protagonist of a new world order.

You have a right to your own opinion, but you cannot say that what I am about to tell you here in the next hour is not the truth.

Today the world population of about six billion people is governed by six thousand elite individuals.

These six thousand individuals consist of government leaders; few heads of international movements; the pope of the Catholic Church; entrepreneurs (Rothschilds, Rockefellers); politicians to minority power broker status; leaders in international business and finance; and the defense industry heads. These six thousand individuals move freely into high positions in their nations' governments and back to private life largely beyond the notice of elected legislatures.

Some US Congress men and women remain uninformed of world affairs beyond the United States borders. Their continual ignorance about what is going on around the world is evident in their unrealistic approaches to social, economic, and political problems in United States and around the world, which is now calling for a new world order to be implemented at a faster speed. I love America because in it I have the freedom to be free and work for freedom and liberty of this one-world government.

The six-thousand superclass that rules our lives on this planet today does have disproportionate influence over every national policy based on their own self-interest across the world. These six thousand individuals support corruption and oppressive governments, provided they can do business in a country where a corrupted and oppressive system is going on. They can support a regime as long as it goes well with their self-interest, so there is no permanent friend or foe but self-interest, notwithstanding how many human lives went into the cemetery in the process.

This agenda of a new world order began a long time ago with the formation of the US Federal Reserve System in 1913, which was a design to control the whole world through economic power in order to measure a sovereign nation by the value of its currency within the parameter of the League of Nations, which officially came into existence in 1919. This idea was strengthened by the establishment of the International Monetary Fund in 1944. After the economic control of nations was established, it gave way to a centralized diplomatic political control with the establishment of the United Nations in 1945, which we all exist to rubber stamp the interest of the security council member nations; what they don't want, they veto.

Once political control and economic control finally got settled in the pocket of the few powerful individuals, they went ahead to set up the World Bank in 1945 and the World Health Organization in 1948 to placate the poor. And when the experiment of the one-world government seemed to be off track, the European Union and the euro currency was put in place in 1993, followed by the World Trade Organization in 1998. In order not to be too late to join them after a hundred years of being alienated in the game plan, the African Union came into being in 2002, followed by the Union of South American Nations in 2008.

When United States realized that the agenda of its one-world government that began in 1913 was no longer classified top secret information, the ruling class moved toward the formation of North American Union and the Amero currency behind the scene by the Council on Foreign Relations in agreement with its counterparts in Mexico and Canada by bypassing the American public and Congress, who have no clues of what is going on in this planet outside their local constituency. The next agenda from 2012 to 2016 is that a new group of international elites may replace the federal government of the United States with a transnational government, which will eventually erase the borders between Mexico, Canada, and the United States.

The ultimate goal of the Council on Foreign Relations is to replace national leaders of governments in Washington, Ottawa, and Mexico

City with a European-style political union style bureaucracy. If this experiment becomes successful through a manipulated political process by the gang of political elites from 2012 to 2016, the People's Republic of China will bury their fear and mistrust of the United States, which will lead to the birth of the Asian Union. Then the world will pressed for a new international reserve currency, and the United Nations Conference on Trade and Development the expansion of IMF's special drawing rights. The United States will end up supporting the adoption of a single global currency for a new world order after the fall in value of the US dollar in regard to oil and energy trading; failure to support this experiment will bankrupt the United States because of its dependence on foreign oil.

A new world order that is in the making must focus on the creation of a world of democracy, peace, and prosperity for all. A comprehensive peace must be grounded in United Nations Security Council Resolutions 242 and 338 and the principle of territory for peace.

This principle must be elaborated to provide for Israel's security and recognition and, at the same time, for legitimate Palestinian political rights and a Palestinian state existing side by side with Israel. Anything else would fail the twin tests of fairness and security. The time has come to put an end to the Arab-Israeli conflict.

We can see a new world coming into view in the Middle East and Africa with revolutions in Tunisia, Egypt, and Libya.

A world order in which the principles of justice and fair play protect the weak against the strong. A world in which freedom and respect for human rights find a home among all nations.

If we do not follow the dictates of our inner moral compass and stand up for human life in 2011, then lawlessness will threaten the peace and democracy of the emerging new world order we now see. We are all the same human beings—blacks, whites, Arabs, Jews, Gentiles, Afrikaans, etc. Therefore, it is quite natural that when some human brothers and sisters suffer, other brothers and sisters spontaneously develop some kind of sincere feeling or concern; we must all consider this a hope for the future that the next century will be a nicer and friendlier one.

What begins in our world in 2011 as signaled by the Arab revolution is an opportunity to utilize our human intelligence and determination to solve mankind's social, economic, and political problems, because this problem is basically a human-created one. In order to solve this problem, the answer must come from humanity itself. With the Internet, the world is becoming smaller and smaller every day, which calls for the new world order to be based on principles of compassion, freedom, and the salvation of humanity through a holistic principle. The new world order will consist of communities of nations, each bound together by religion and culture and joined in economic and political relationships to substantiate a world of peace and take positive steps to make harmony with each other's religious differences and belief systems.

It is my God-ordained mission to bring the world to unity under God and put an end to a world of selfish individuals oppressing others for their own pleasure. Only a few people have followed the voice of conscience emanating from their mind, which teaches them to pursue truth, beauty, and goodness and to resist the temptations of the body, materialism, and oppression of others in pursuit of wealth and monetary gains. Only the people that help the poor, the sick, and the needy among us can meet God and find heaven on earth and peace in their soul. When the religious leaders have united for the sake of world peace under God, the politicians will obey the teachings of religion. Then and only then will the social and economic problems be solved, when the world's religions unite on the path of peace.

To ensure a well-rounded education for individuals and close communication between all segments of society in the role and involvement of the academic and religious communities is very necessary.

People must constantly cooperate with one another in order to raise up individuals who can develop civilized families, churches, schools, and societies.

Extreme poverty and wealth can no longer be reconciled in the society of mankind; governments that come into power through democratic elections must serve the electorate rather than their corporate donors.

The greatest task of our generation is the problem of implementing well-rounded education and eradicating illiteracy in our pluralistic global village. The new world order will provide a formula based on the majority rule, respect for human rights, and global peaceful participation; and the United Nations must be empowered to prevent international aggression and human rights violations by one nation against another or by a leader against his own citizens. In any nation, political or economic or religious perpetrators must be brought to justice and pay the ultimate price for their wicked actions or be forced to provide remedy to the victims.

Participation of a nation in international affairs is not a right but a privilege that must be earned by proper domestic and international conduct.

Therefore, isolation and sanctions are tools to deal with nations who are working against the peace of this global village we call our planet. Hinduism, Buddhism, Confucianism, Judaism, Christianity, and Islam must work together to boost global cooperation and respect for human rights based on the majority rule and respect for human rights with emphasis on the importance of education, population policy, refugees, homelessness, and global health-care services.

My idea of a one-world government is simply an order where all the nations of the world will be treated the same way the states are treated within the United States of America.

I am a protagonist of a new world order where disputes between nations will be handled in a court situation rather than the battlefield. The international government will supersede the existing international structure. It will not attempt to change what already exists within a nation. Issues, such as the environment, will be handled by experts from all over the world, who will make up the departments of the one-world government. Shared research will ensure that solutions to the issues will be found. Every nation, culture, religion, and individual has the right to be respected. The economic aspect will be based on win-win agreements, with every nation finding its niche based on its natural resources.

The international government that I am proposing will handle the balance of trade and ensure that a nation's natural resources benefit the people. International oil and gas pipelines across nations, a world in which nations without oil and gas will benefit in royalty payment for allowing gas and oil pipelines across their national territory from there through here to there to form a global energy supply network on this single commodity that is dividing all of us. I dream of a new world order where one day Israel will see itself fulfilling an obligation of brotherhood in the Abrahamic religion of Christianity, Islam, and Judaism, with Israel becoming a supply of electricity and the essential needs of life across a no-wall border to a Palestine state where the sons and daughters of both Christians and Muslims, Jews and Arabs will sit together in a coffee shop of brotherhood.

I have a dream of a day that will come very soon across the Israel-Palestine border where no longer the scene of machine guns angry and confused. Border patrol soldiers are no longer required. A new day when United States military contractors will come back home and turn their weapons into tools for mechanized farming in North America to feed the world, no longer to police the world as policemen for Judeo-Christians. That is my dream.

The September 11 attacks is said by some as a false flag operation carried out by the United States intelligence community as part of a strategy of tension to justify political repression at home and preemptive war abroad and the transition of the United States to a police state.

The hidden agenda of the few elite to create a surveillance in order to be in control of the new world order was the reason for the unnecessary wars we witnessed in Iraq and Afghanistan, which was just to justify the gang of super elites in government and private sectors to do what they got to do to escape the critics and placate popular opinion in setting up mass surveillance at airports, streets, and phones; regulating the social media against "Wikileaking" their behind-the-scene operations; using Social Security numbers to regulate the citizens; using of credit ratings through the credit bureaus and the banking systems to stereotype some races out of economic power and real estate ownership through FICO (Fair Isaac Corporation) scores; and using the FICO scores credit rating monster to regulate the growing educated middle class from becoming a threat to the superclass elite club.

Very soon, microchip implants will assist corporations and the government to track every move of consumers and citizens. As the right steps toward the one-world sociopolitical economic order, these steps are necessary to bypass a few elements in United States Congress, who think the world revolves around the community they represent in the Congress and may want to make noise using Western media campaign to derail this agenda of one-world government, which began in 1913. The United States is ruled from behind the scenes by a small secretive group that wants to change the government system and put the country under the control of a world government. The tool of this game is the financialization of the economy, Today, without money, you cannot be a head of government unless you get a donation or sponsorship from members of the super rich, elite club.

Regulation and restriction of poor communities and poor nations of our world are done through speech control, media propaganda, cold war agenda, through the concentration of media ownership in the hands of members of the six-thousand club is fixed. Through mass surveillance and widespread use of state terrorism, the government can now shut down protesters' view points and legitimate aspirations; shut down social media, phone systems, and websites; and buy up staff and management employees at Facebook and Wikimedia to control information of who is who and which is which. What will poor people and poor nations do if all means of communication and media are now in the hand of the six-thousand elite club? They can allow naked teenagers on social media sites, but you cannot post any truth statements because truth is classified information.

The encompassing propaganda through a cult of personality around a chosen sponsored puppet president in the White House and nations' government around the world through their manipulated electoral system, which appears has the voice of the people, but we all know 80 percent of the time is always the interest of corporate leaders.

Members of the Congress receive loans from them to campaign for the position they now occupy. In democracy, such a loan is called donation. If so, why can't someone donate to me? Because they know I will not represent their own selfish agenda, but the citizens of the world.

To attain the goal of one-world government is to establish the role of new emerging major zonal powers that in any way will still make the United States as one of the unchallengeable arbiters of world affairs. The United States will no longer be the only superpower as we see it today. American citizens may not like this idea, seeing United States losing its policeman position of the world, but what can we do about it, folks? Nothing when you are now broke, fighting back debt ceiling and budget cuts at home, because whosoever has its name printed on the new currency of the coming one-world government will control the new world order, and no longer will it be only the members of the security council to rule this world.

The mass media and church leaders are now busy playing their part in the manufacturing of a national consensus and, paradoxically, a culture of fear for increased social and religious control that a mistrustful and mutually fearing population might offer to those in power.

The religious leaders now working to oppose the formation of a one-world government have settled for a principle of controlling the mind-set of a vast majority of people. That is why the same principle will be used to push forward the idea of the new world order, which will be implemented through the use of mind control with a broad range of tactics able to subvert an individual's control of his or her own thinking and behavior put in place by preachers themselves, because whosoever has the money that sponsors the preachers will be able to use the preachers, so the protagonist of one-world government will use not only the entertainment industry to keep the mind-set of people playing while we are working toward our goal and objectives of one-world government.

The seed of the new social, economic, and political order sown into the mind of people through sports, entertainment, and programmed lifestyles is enough already to make the sermons of preachers a mere fall onto dry ground and render ineffective the Abrahamic religious leaders of Islam, Christianity, and Judaism who have determined to manipulate the democratic election process in favor of politicians as spoilers of this one-world government in the making.

Today we live in a world where anyone who has an opinion or thought of his own different from the government of the day, political agenda, or ideas opposite to popular religious leaders' interpretation of the Bible is considered as a terrorist or labeled as the anti-Christ or called a funny name like a racist or anti-Semitist.

No biblical scholar will deny the fact that Jesus Christ is the Prince of Peace, for the book of Isaiah 9:6–7 says, "For unto us a child is born, the government shall be upon his shoulder, his name shall be call the Prince of peace, the increase of his government and peace, there shall be no end." That is why, at the end of Jesus's ministry on earth, he told his disciples, "Go ye to all the world and make disciples of all nations, my peace I leave with you, love your neighbors as you love yourself, without peace no one can see God." So the one singular assignment of a Christian on this planet is to bring all mankind back to God—the Jews, Arabs, Afrikaans, Asians, Americans, British, etc.—and establish a government of peace, prosperity, freedom, and liberty on earth. It is this principle of peace, liberty, and freedom for all mankind and good government in our world communities that inspired me to establish the organization Center for Religious Peace and New World Order.

The coming one-world government will consist of about six unions:

1. African Union
2. European Union
3. North American Union
4. Asian Union
5. South American Union
6. Union of the Arab League

The new world order will emerge after the dust has settled on the ongoing Middle East Arab revolution, which will lead the United Nations to take stand on Israel and Palestinian statehood for peace in a way that will usher in the fall of immigration walls between the Mexico border and United States and Canada for a common currency under the North American Union.

Once the North American Union becomes publicly acceptable to the majority of the citizens, there will be a frustrated exodus of African immigrants in diaspora back to their homeland, Africa; and Jews will have two homelands, Israel and the United States of America, alienated from the Asian Union. Until the religious leaders facilitate peace within the parameter of the Abrahamic order of Islam, Christianity, and Judaism, which will finally establish peace in the Middle East, the peace we desire may not come from the politicians but from religious leaders using interfaith conflict resolution to back up politicians' desire for world peace. Blessed are the peacemakers, for they shall be called the children of God. Peace will come when those who are called the children of God are mature enough to forget their own personal interests and employ their calling by God and their anointing to bring peace to our world. United Nations employees are working for their money, but religious leaders are accounted to God. Peace in our world is their responsibility; we will have peace when the religious leaders of the Abrahamic faith of Judaism, Islam, and Christianity come to a table of brotherhood to help politicians out in achieving world peace.

If perfection were by Leviticus priesthood for which under the people received Mosaic law, what further need was there that another priest should rise after the order of Melchisedec and not after the order of Aaron? But because the priesthood has been changed by God, there is made a necessary change from the Mosaic law given to one tribe, the Jewish people. Despite the fact that Jesus Christ sprang out of Judah (a Jewish tribe), he was made a priest not after the order of Aaron (a Jew) but after the order of Melchisedec, the king of peace. Therefore, whosoever is against peace in our world and refuses to compromise in the Middle East to give peace a chance is not a child of God but a terrorist, and such person or group or nation cannot claim that actions of violence and bloodshed of innocent women and children is supported by God. The imam, the pastors, the rabbis owe the world a duty in interfaith conflict resolution to bring peace to the Middle East.

The faith traditions offer significant resources for healing broken relationships at the personal, community, national, and international levels. Leaders of faith communities must rise up to become effective managers of conflict resolution around the world, because the politicians have failed the world in handling the Middle East affairs. The social and economic inequality that you see everywhere in our world today was created and perpetuated to date by both religious leaders and politicians in that church and Islam had historically been connected to the hierarchy of political authority because they became part of it during the colonial times. This hierarchy of political authority associated with the cleric hierarchy basically was what established a symbiotic relationship of power and controlling society, so it was religious leaders who always want to put their faith in a position of preserving and seeking to preserve their own thought of school of how God should be worshiped that legitimatized military repression and autocratic leaders in many nations. They would tell the indigenous people to accept the poor social and economic conditions in which they were immersed by the few because they will find heaven.

In another life, the streets are made with gold. Diamond and dollars you donate in the temple or drop in the mosque are saved for you when you go to heaven; so, brethren, accept the way things are because at the end of the day, you will inherit heaven. So if we have to change this world and create a new world order of peace, the same religious leaders have to be part of the conflict resolution as a third party to politicians. I love America because in it I have the freedom to be free and work for freedom and liberty of a one-world government. Judaism and Sharia laws made nothing perfect for centuries in our world because you cannot legislate morality. It is against human nature to legislate morality. You have to speak to human minds with love and dialogue. That is why the bringing in of a better hope by Jesus Christ's teaching and principles of love and peace between man and God and between one another, which is the only way by which we all can draw nigh to God in a new world order that is in the making, is the only option left to achieve reconciliation and peace. In the Bible, Jesus says, "My peace I give unto you." Be at peace with all men; without peace, no one can see God. How then, you tell me, can God support your use of machine guns and force to kill women and children because of occupation of lands?

The book of Psalms 122:6 says, "Pray for the Peace of Jerusalem." God did not tell us to go and kill Muslim brotherhood but to pray for the Jews. The Bible did not say put black men in prisons to give job to prison contractors of California. The Bible says peace be within the walls of Jerusalem. What walls was the Bible talking about? The walls built about three thousand years ago? Or the one currently being built by the politicians as a possible border of demarcation of the Jewish state and the Palestine state? Which one in our changing world should we pray for? The Bible says, they that love thy walls shall prosper. It's not talking about they that love the Jews and hate the Iranians or Iraqis or hate those poor, frustrated Taliban members who need medicine for their health-care needs. Pray for the Jews and curse the poor and needy who live under the caves, behind used iron curtains in a cold weather?

The Taliban live in desert winter, summer, and spring on the mountains and the valley with rattle snakes and animals. Their houses are in the region of holes and caves. Who sold them machine guns? Who are buying their locally made cocaine under the rock? Where did their guns come from? And where did the cocaine get exported to? Those human beings who are in a desert, in dusty bamboo houses made with palm tree roofing sheets does not need your gospel, humanitarian help but the Jews only?

In an attempt to eliminate Rwanda's Tutsi minority, the Hutu majority systematically slaughtered eight hundred thousand individuals—most of them civilians—in just one hundred days, a rate of killing that rivals the worst in human history. Armed with machetes, the killers were both vicious and organized, torturing their victims, murdering them in cold blood, and dumping their bodies in mass graves. The Rwandan genocide is worse than the genocide of Nazi Germany.

The genocide of eight hundred thousand African men, women, and children in one hundred days. How did the international community respond? How did the Jews who had a similar experience under Hitler respond? They then were busy doing the same thing to other people across the border somewhere with the support of United States Congress.

What the Bible is talking about is that those who love peace will prosper, so the assignment given to me as a Christian is to pray for the peace of Jerusalem, loves the peace of Jerusalem, and work toward peace within and around a new border that will stand to establish peace and the statehood of Israel and Palestine toward a new world order of peace. Then prosperity will come to our world. This is a duty for religious leaders who want to be blessed and be named as children of God.

"Whosoever blesses Israel will be blessed, and whosoever curses Israel will be cursed" is just a biblical jargon that has been perpetuated for too long by church leaders in prayer meeting clubs. What the Bible said was to pray for the peace of Jerusalem; whosoever loves his peace and loves his wall shall prosper. God is prospering me because I love peace. I am a professional peacemaker, and because I do this God-assigned duty, I am a child of God. You will be out of your mind to call me anti-Semitic, which anyway is just a term for people with a funny language; and no one has a funnier, more difficult language with an accent than me, so I too am a Semite. If you hate me because of my accent, you are anti-Semitic. How about that?

It is when the United Nations comes up with a bold declaration, action, and support for a peaceful wall between the two, making Palestine the 194th member of United Nations, that International Monetary Fund and debts here and there, which are crippling world economy, will turn around into prosperity for all. So what we should all work and pray for is not the Jews but peace in Israel. There are no Jews or Gentiles or Arabs in the gospel of our Lord Jesus Christ but salvation for all mankind and peace in our world. The time has come for us to put an end to these false preachers and teachers manipulating the interpretation of the Bible to manipulate American and Israeli politicians to prevent the United Nations from achieving peace as desired and commanded by God. Church members residing in ghetto Compton praying for Jews in Beverly Hills, California? Come on, give me a break. That is the kind of prayer meeting you have in your church. No wonder nobody came again.

Pray for the peace of Jerusalem, not the Jews. Pray for walls, not Israel, so that peace be established in a way that both sides will agree on a wall that will be the border between the two nations, a peaceful wall that will recognize both Israel and Palestine's statehood in comity of nations toward the coming one-world government.

Prayer points are peace for walls and peace about West and East Jerusalem because now the Arab League is asking for the West as the capital of Palestine, and Netanyahu has built an unauthorized and unacceptable wall already, which will make any peace plan now temporary. Tear down this wall and build a new wall acceptable to United Nations in accordance to the principle of religious peace and new world order.

2 CHAPTER NAME

Israel and Palestine Conflict Resolution

The patriarch Abraham is a faithful friend of God and father of the Hebrew nation. He is called father of the faithful. He had one wife, Sarah, and two baby mamas, Hagar and Keturah.

"And Sarah Abram's wife took Hagar her maid the Egyptian, and gave her to her husband Abram to be his wife" (Gen. 16:3). "Then again Abraham took a wife, and her name was Keturah" (Gen. 25:1). Sarah was the mother of Isaac, Hagar was the mother of Ishmael and was an Egyptian, and Keturah was a black woman. Isaac became the nation of Israel,

Ishmael became the nation of Arab (note that his mother was from Egypt), and Keturah's children moved down West Africa and became my fathers of men and women taken by slaves to the new world. Now let's have a run-through of the origin of the problem of Israel and Palestine conflict.

Israel and Arab conflicts in relation to Egypt and to what may be the views of some black people in this global family problem modern days see only from the view of as just a border war between Israel and the Middle East. Isaac became the father of Jacob, but God changed Jacob's name to Israel on the day God passed by Brother Jacob's night prayer meeting chapel. Jacob was just a guy that was getting tired running around the world as a Jew in Diaspora from his home country, having to work fourteen years in a foreign country to save enough money to marry the lady of his dreams, and when he finally did, he lost the woman in childbirth due to lack of health insurance at the local maternity clinic. So Jacob challenged God to a wrestling match one day. God showed up in the local church's night prayer vigil. Since then, God never came to anybody's prayer meeting like a man again. Now God comes unseen, never again to be seen by man because there are many Jacobs coming to prayer meetings these days. Jacob started this wrestling match with God that if he doesn't get blessed that night and get what he wants, he will let God go back to heaven. That was the day God blessed him and changed his name from Jacob to Israel, so *Israel* simply means fighting with God and everybody for what you want by occupation or by force, taking what belongs to others to add to your own to satisfy your own selfish interest, and you end up saying it was God who took it from others and gave it to you because God loves you more than your brother next door, and until you get it, you will not respect any spiritual order or authority in this world, even if you end up with a walking stick, fighting to get what you want at all cost.

Ishmael, the other child of Abraham from his baby mama, was sent out of the house with his mother with no child support from Abraham, who was rich with silver and gold. He only gave Ishmael one ninety-nine-cent bottle of water on the day he sent the boy out into Arabian desert because

Sarah, the legal wife, demanded the boy and the mother be sent away from this rich man's house, all because the baby mama operated under her fundamental human right of free speech to have an attitude and just say her mind about how she feels being in her baby daddy's house. That was why later, God of Justice compensated Ishmael's experience of having to be raised by a single mother with a vast land of oil reserve in the Arabian Desert, which the world now knows today as oil from the Middle East.

Another grandchild of Abraham's baby mama Keturah left home too and settled in another part of Africa. Remember, his grandmother was a black woman from North Africa and Ishmael's mother was from Egypt, but the favored son grandchild a the favored boy by name Israel become the chieftain of Habiru people, set to fulfill what God promised to his father, Abraham, as recorded in Genesis chapter 11, that he (God) will make him a nation. These three sons from three different baby mamas today are still serving the monotheistic God of their father but in three different religious methods of worship: Judaism, Christianity, and Islam.

From my little story, you can now see that the problem of our world is nothing more than a family problem that the present generation is fighting only from the perception of a religious warfare. When God promised Abraham to make him a nation, a promise that Abraham's children will be numerous, six billion people like the sand of the sea or two million people in Israel regulated state? Was God talking only about the Jews and the tiny plot of land of Israel state and Palestine state or one nation of the world that encompasses both the Jews and the Gentiles?

A nation in the mind of God is not a geographical location but a people. Israel is a people. It is not Jerusalem that made them a people; they were already a nation before they crossed the Red Sea from Egypt to their presently occupied territory. The twelve spies told us in the Bible that giants were living in that location before they started the occupation of the territory thousands of years ago led by a spy called Joshua, who became their leader after the death of Moses. It is not the present land of Israel that made the Jews a people loved and chosen by God, but God chose the Jews as his own people even before they got to where the dome is built now, so you don't lose your identity or relationship with God because of eviction from your apartment by the landlord.

Eviction by a bank because of foreclosure or car repossession has nothing to do with your losing your salvation or relationship with God. God cannot be measured by a plot of land or movable or immovable properties or earthly possession, so for people to be playing a self-defense propaganda that God supported them for sticking to a plot of land is beneath the glory and power of the God of this universe. When you sign a mortgage to buy a house at the age of sixty-five and promise to pay it back in thirty years, and you later refinanced the house for another additional fifteen years on your seventieth birthday anniversary—70 plus 45, which means you promised to pay up the mortgage at 115 years old—you know you are just playing games with the banking system and international monetary families. How many members of your family live up to ninety years old?

The day you signed this agreement at the escrow, you knew this thing is just a game of the world. But you got to do what you got to do if that is what everybody wants you to do in order not to become homeless and at least put your name in title of something. Now you want God to come down from heaven with his angels to change Bank of America and the International Monetary Family? God has his own game plan; his agenda is to save all mankind, not only the Jews.

You don't lose whom God has made you by losing a land or a job or a car. Blessed is the peacemaker, for they shall be called the children of God. What will you do if a peacemaker like me is called a child of God? What do you call someone who refuses to accept peace or give up a land for peace? A child of God too? My friends, we are all strangers and pilgrims on earth.

The nation and children that God promised Abraham is the six billion of mankind, not just the 0.02 percent of the Jews and Palestinians who want to break the necks of the rest of the world unless they have what they want or else we will not have peace in our world.

The Jews became a people, a nation through trials of cruel mocking and scoring, wars, bonds, and imprisonment, wandering about in sheepskins and goatskins, being destitute, afflicted, tormented, and persecuted in gas chambers, just like the Negro in America; so it was not West Jerusalem or Gaza or a landed property that made them a nation. So fighting for a land with Palestine or neighbors paying the Taliban, al-Qaeda, or terrorists back in their own coin is not a spiritual and godly response to evil and good diplomacy. It is just political and military hegemony propaganda by the Yankee congressmen and congresswomen and the Zionist politicians in the Middle East. The time to put a stop to this nonsense in our world is now.

I am not looking for approval of politicians for this message. I have no special interest in this case as a peacemaker, and you don't have to like me since I am not like Pastor John Hagee, a San Antonio–based preacher with some superstitious ideas about Israel and the rest of the world. And that is not to say that I am against the Christian Zionist movement. No one supports Israel more than I do because I read my King James Bible too: "Negro Slaves Obey your white Master." (*Negro* means "black" in Spanish anyway.) It's not a bad thing to call a black man a Negro. *In Sha Allah* means "by the grace of God" in the Arab language, so there is nothing wrong for a Christian to say *In Sha Allah*. Anyway, why I am different from other religious leaders is because I read more books besides the Bible and Koran or Torah, and my assignment in this world is different from that of the Apostle Associations of Bishops (APAC), and I am what I am by the grace of God.

If anybody says God is for him, he is for me too. He sent me here to do this job of a new world order, and I will accomplish my purpose and destiny before I shed the coat of mortality for immortality. God has made me one of the instruments of his wishes in the power of the gift of the Holy Spirit given to me by his grace, and I believe in the gospel of Jesus Christ. Therefore, I take this assignment toward religious peace and new world order not by the standard of pride of a place in history or for personal glory or profit, but I am just happy to be part of the group of chosen men in my generation set to establish a new world order bringing man back to God and establishing peace, security, human rights, and economic prosperity in our world, a world nothing less to be called by all than a kingdom of God here on earth where peace shall reign.

The world is awaiting the coming of the children of the highest God to fix our broken world system.

I will not shy away from saying to you that God has anointed me with oil of gladness among my fellows, and I have come in the volume of words to initiate the will of God on earth and lay a foundation on an already established secret agenda that will usher in the dialogue toward a new world order where liberty and justice shall reign on earth. A day is coming. Behold, it is at hand when there will be a new Jerusalem—not the current one where you go for yearly holy pilgrimage that we are told to pray for and preserved by the Yankee preachers and Zionist prophets. Jesus will not come down to rule in a Jerusalem built with the blood of innocent women and children across the Gaza Strip. He prefers to come down with his own mobile home and name it a new Jerusalem, a new city of the living God on earth, a new Mount Zion, the city of the coming King, the joy and center of our blessing.

In the new Jerusalem—not this one where you go for vacation every year all because you have the money for a travel ticket. I am talking about a city being prepared by Jesus that will descend like a mobile home from heaven, where there will be Emmanuel Tula and all peace-loving people playing around with an innumerable company of holy angels walking on the city of gold with the cherubim and the seraphim. Not this one in Palestine, stained with the blood of Jews and Arabs, Muslims and Christians, innocent women and children across the Israeli prime minister's illegal fence. Not the one with police checkpoints by Israeli and Hamas leaders. Ladies and gentlemen, I am talking about a new Jerusalem prepared by the only one Mediator between man and God, the second Adam: Jesus Christ, who, by a new covenant, is coming back very soon to establish a new kingdom on earth.

When this present East and West Jerusalem wall and border in Israel shall pass away, until then, brothers, let us have peace in our world.

The Architect and the Builder of this new Jerusalem is coming back again. He is not like Moslem Brotherhood or Gospel Sisters in the Spirit, taking sides between two brothers of Abraham's different baby mamas, because before Abraham was, he was. How then, you say to me, you have Abraham as father of Israel? Even your father Abraham rejoiced for the day he was set at the right hand of God. God's promise to Abraham is a nation—a new world order in the making, a one-world government where the ruler himself shall be God. Let brotherly love begin now in the Middle East, entertain strangers among you, take care of those Arabs who are refugees among you; and for those who suffer the adversity of homelessness and hunger, Jesus has made a sacrifice for peace with his own blood on the cross of Calvary. Shedding the blood of men, women, and children for land occupation by terrorists of one nation to favor another is a war Jesus will not support on his second return to this world.

The Jews have no longer a continued ownership of the whole city of Jerusalem but should begin to seek the new one to come already built like a mobile home by the Prince of Peace. It will descend from heaven with paid mortgage as a gift to mankind without Bank of America's monthly interest bills. There all his followers who love peace shall be, for before Jesus went away, he said "My peace I give unto you," but not as machine guns and border fencing can give you. How then would he support a nation or a people or troublemaking politicians in a standing ovation to wars, those educated millionaires seeking reelection with Jewish campaign donations in United States Congress, capitalizing on Obama truth to Jews? Those who have no time to read the Bible for themselves but are supporting the rejection of the peace plan of the United Nations can have their own opinion and take sides, but God has given me the ministry of reconciliation to bring all mankind everywhere back to God in a one-world government. May the peace of God be with me and you too. *In Sha Allah.*

New World Order THE TOWER OF BABEL

The most honorable assignment in this world is the ministry of truth, and it is a dangerous assignment that God has given me, which I will do here before you today based on the first sentence of the US Declaration of Independence: "A decent respect to the opinions of mankind." What I am about to say is my own opinion. Whosoever disagrees with my own ideas or opinions is free to offer a better alternative instead of responding with a negative form of hatred from a bully pulpit of his or her own religious denomination to justify that the world population of six billion people should continue to be under the corporate economic and political manipulation of the six thousand super elite among us.

These six thousand individuals consist of government leaders; a few heads of international movements; the pope of the Catholic church and a few powerful religious denominational leaders; entrepreneurs like Rockefellers; politicians to minority power broker status; leaders in international business, finance, and banking; and the defense industry heads.

These six thousand individuals move freely into high positions in their nation's government and back to private life largely beyond the notice of the electorate, who are manipulated to keep reelecting same old folks over and over again, which is what God wanted to prevent in the first instance when he scattered them away from building the Tower of Babel. God was not against the idea of a one-world government but against the idea of autocratic leadership of Nimrod and the few elites who want to steal mankind's freedom and liberty to have access to God's goodness and provision scattered around the lands of this planet.

It is important to note that although chapter 10 of Genesis precedes the account of Babel in chapter 11, the events described in both chapters are not rendered in a chronologically consecutive fashion. Accordingly, it must be understood that the tenth chapter of Genesis details events prior, during, and after those described in chapter 11.

Genesis chapter 10 is specifically written to demonstrate that all humanity descended from Noah, who was a virtuous man in the eyes of God (Gen. 6:8–9). It is reasonable to presume that the commandments of God were passed on to his sons. Genesis chapter 10 verses 5, 20, and 32 also suggest that the land of the earth was physically divided at this time in response to Babel. There was the Tower of Babel incident before the Flood during Noah's days. The book of Genesis specifies: "The name of the one Noah 3 Sons was Peleg, for in his days the earth was divided" (Gen. 10:25). *Peleg* means "division." The coastal outlines of the earth's continents suggest the likely prior unification of the various land masses. The terra firma can be viewed as a once-unified puzzle now separated into its various fragments after the flood as the waters was finding a way to get back to the ocean after Noah in order to dry up the land.

When God first created the earth, you could jump in your car and drive from Los Angeles to Nigeria because there were no islands, no rivers to cross, no land separated with water. But it was after the flood during Noah son by the name of *Peleg* (which means "divisions") that the planet was divided into islands, continents, etc., that you will need bridges, boats and ships, or airplanes to cross from one place to the other. But in the beginning of creation, God wanted man to walk from one point to as far as he can go because his original plan was not that if you were born in Cuba, you should live and die in Cuba and not be allowed to travel out of Cuba by Castro Sr. or Castro Jr., just like Nimrod wanted to do in the Babel village.

On the fifth day of the creation of the earth, God gave this command to the birds and fishes (Gen. 1:20–23). On the sixth day, God reiterated this command to the pinnacles of creation, man and woman (Gen.1:26–28). Humanity was to subjugate the untamed earth by dispersing themselves.

The builders in Shinar banded themselves together for a common ecumenical purpose (under one pastor and his church team): to pursue a project of building a cathedral, a mosque, a dome, or as the Bible calls it, a tower in the village of Babel. A religious ambition of one man and his cartel of elders around him to convince everybody that what they set to do is the will of God and will benefit everybody. Everybody buys into it in unity without any opposing views allowed. Somebody must have prayed to God to come down; he or she probably did not belong to the deacon and elder council to protest, but he or she could pray to God about the autocratic leadership.

What is the difference between Muammar Gaddafi, who rules Libyan people for forty-two years and wants to go only on the condition that he be allowed to leave the leadership of his own people in his own country for his own son to succeed him, until his own people carried out a revolution to remove him from power? Same autocratic leadership we all witnessed in our generation in Egypt, Syria, Saudi Arabia, etc., in comparison to what is going on among us church founders today?

Pastors who lead his own church for forty-two years, build his own congregation, and want to retire from preaching at eighty-two only on the condition to be allowed to leave the pulpit for his own son or son-in-law or his daughter? And just like in Syria, Libya, Egypt, Saudi Arabia, politicians and pastors' similarity in leadership is a demonstration that man by nature is autocratic but not a democratic being. Therefore, in order to save the people from a clique of super elite elders or influential charismatic leaders in this planet who have nothing to offer but good oratorical speeches to keep mankind running around a mountain for forty years until they all die waiting for a better life that only their children may live to see in the next generation—that is why we now live a world where people across all nations of the world must save themselves through a government of democracy to stop the kind of autocratic leadership where a man with his chosen super elite class will be the person that will order us all what best to do, when to go, where to go, when to stop, when to do this or that. What he thinks is good for all people because it is good for him. If it's good for you, then it must be accepted by me, or else I am a rebel, a Judas, anti-Christ, anti-Semitist, anti-American, anti-this, and anti-that who must be prayed out of the church by sisters in the spirit through 24-7 prayer intercessors chains—all because I have an opinion that seems to oppose Pastor Nimrod. And all the people respectfully honor and agree with the elder's directions with no opposition to his own self-centered ambition because he presented it to us all as if it was God's plan for all of us. Till today, politicians still use God's books (like the Bible, Koran, and Torah) to take people's votes for elections. That is what happened in Libya, in Egypt, in Tunisia, in Syria, in Saudi Arabia, and in the village of Babel, where one man and his super elite class led the whole mankind to build a cathedral Tower of Babel. God is not an autocratic leader. He rules the universe by rules, regulations, natural and spiritual laws set in place; and God obeys such rules himself. That is why, most of the time, God does not answer the prayer of most men.

You cannot pray God to violate his own laws. If you violate it, he may forgive you, but the forces set in place against violators will catch up with you later on the way. That is why you are still suffering today for the bad decisions or bad choices you made in the past. God forgave you, but he cannot violate the principle of his universal natural and spiritual laws, which suggests to you that he may not be autocratic like Gadhafi as you have been told by your pastor or imam. Through his son, Jesus Christ, God forced no salvation on any man. He gives us the choice to choose, though preachers may convince us that God practices autocracy because the Gospel is presented as such to us, but God demonstrated to us at the Tower of Babel that such system of leadership is not the best for this planet. That was one of the reasons he destroyed the Tower of Babel, where a man and his chosen elders decided to manipulate everybody within the village through media propaganda to stay put in a Babylonian small village and be shut out from traveling out to another land and become limited in their own thinking and mind-set.

Some nationals who never travel out of their city behave to other immigrants as if the whole planet was the size of their own county. They are cut off for their lifetime, not knowing that the world is bigger than building a Tower of Babel in Babel village, that only the pastor, first lady, and his son at the end of the day will be allowed by the security guards to get to the top of the dome after the contractors hand over the keys. The rest of the congregation (99 percent) will never know what is kept at the top of the tower anymore, and that is the tower built by all of us, just like Jones village where the pastor set up a bed to teach teenage girls under eighteen how to perform well during sex on bed as pastors' spiritual wives. Homosexuals priests at the cathedral tower with boys and girls who, after the acts, will descend down from the cathedral tower to the pulpit to give Holy Communion to the rest of the members of Jones Babel village. And when we were burning the brick with our own mortgage payments and car payments by notes and paychecks, when you preached us above the gifts of our tithes and offering, Apostle Nimrod said to us that all of us will be using it to climb up and down to heaven to talk to God. But now after the dedication of the dome, this cathedral Tower of Babel, the church security guards only allow Pastor Nimrod Jr. to climb up there.

God knew that the Tower of Babel at the end of the day was the ambition of one man using the others' superstitious, religious mentality to manipulate all mankind to reach his own goals and objectives and do it in the name of God to benefit himself and his immediate family and make all the rest of the people who contributed their life's savings and volunteered their time in the projects as unpatriotic at the end of the day. And God came down to set up democracy, the government of the people by the people, where votes in a democratic elections are hijacked and manipulated by few autocratic people at the end of the day to set up a Nimrod agenda. But what does man end up doing to man today in the nations of the world where he scattered them? Six billion people are now ruled today by only six thousand individuals. They are back again—tower, cathedral, dome, and mansion builders.

The Tower of Babel builders will use everybody's support and partnership to create a great name for themselves and their family in the name of God's business. They are here again—Tower of Babel builders in the name of serving God and serving the people, autocratic leaders who hate democracy. All they want is to build mansions and to have a great name to convince the world that in order to talk to God and hear from God, your dome, cathedral, mosque, synagogue, office tower must reach high, and the top must be seen anywhere in the Babel village.

The builders of the Tower of Babel in the book of Genesis conceived their idea outside the propositions of the principle of peace, justice, stable government, benevolent rule, and the admonitions that "the strong may not oppressed the weak," so the ideas behind the builders of the Tower of Babel is what you too will not approve if you were alive in Hammurabi generation. God was not against the unity of mankind and a one-world government but against the idea of Babel village. It was autocratic and not democratic; it looks good but is evil.

The same Babel idea is part of some political or religious denomination philosophy today for leadership. God stopped the project of the Tower of Babel because of the people's bad intentions of world unity based on a wrong proposition for humanity under autocratic rule. The unity of man was a good idea six thousand years ago, and it's what we need now in our world. The evil is between autocracy and democracy. God simply did not want all of mankind to occupy one spot as a city. He wanted them to know he had millions of square miles for mankind to enjoy and explore with minerals and resources for mankind's enjoyment and development. There was no fight for land then between Israel and Palestine. That is why today Hammurabi is celebrated as the founder of internationalism, because of their fundamental principle of the unity of mankind.

You can look it up at the entrance to the General Assembly Hall of United Nations.

Did God come down now to pull down the United Nations building in New York? No. It's still standing because he knows the unity for which God was against. "The republic of the whole world," as proposed or initiated by the Tower of Babel generation, is now needed in the world we are living in today more than ever. This is the right time to come together with one voice, one accord for a one-world government. The Tower of Babel was destroyed because of the people's mind-set of limitation of God's plan for mankind. God has more for them than where they were, but they loved their individualist little village and did not want to embrace the good God's provision of a bigger world, and the few are programming the minds of all not to believe that the world is bigger than what you know and see or are familiar with in your own neighborhood. That is why traveling is part of education, because the intention of God was not to make a man live in a close society under one monarchy with the belief that no other country exists anywhere other than your native land or that there is no other place or better system than yours.

What God was against in the story of the biblical Tower of Babel as recorded in the book of Genesis is the fact of a close society and country or people locked up in isolation by few leaders where one king will end up manipulating the destiny of all in one place, preventing them to go out of the walled country, just like you see in communist states of the world today, like Iran, China, Cuba, Saudi Arabia, etc., or in some religious denomination where founders indoctrinated their own followers not to work with other denominations of same faith or race or nationality. What was Jesus Christ's prayer to his disciples anyway? Let them be one, so God wants unity among mankind, but what he detested in the building of the Tower of Babel was the idea of the possibility of one man building an empire as a king over his own people, which would have ended up preventing God from showing mankind around the world the beauty of his holiness.

With the vast majesty of his creation and the benevolence of his resources he has placed here and there around the world for the

38

benefit of mankind, it is wrong to put that power into one man's empire and his children in a single city to run like a private enterprise. It was not an idea of peace, liberty, and freedom; that was bad to God. It is the opportunity that would have risen by the leaders of the builders of the Tower of Babel, which would lead to the manipulation of 95 percent of the people to the happiness and success of only 5 percent who were privileged religiously, socially, economically, and politically. That is why since then, no empire ever lasted for a century. All men are created equal to have equal rights and live together with each other in peace, liberty, and freedom as free moral agents. Compare this now with the way a government or a religious organization is being managed today in your own backyard.

Those are the religious leaders and government leaders that will oppose today my concept of democratic peace and liberal internationalism to end the era of total war in our world toward my theory as one of the protagonists of a one-world government. The "brotherhood of man" and the "sisterhood of woman." I do not care how many degrees you have. If you have not traveled out of your own country before or were never encouraged the study of world history and geography by your own government, your national leaders are just building the Tower of Babel by putting his own people in isolation from the world through the filtering of information, news, radio, televisions, movies, and music that you can or cannot listen to or watch in your own country; and very soon the wall they built around your people will be torn down in the ongoing process of a new world order for you to see that there is another better thing that God has for you, more than what you are embracing now in your close society, where the information and news about what is going on in other parts of the world is kept from your radio and television set.

Your political and religious leaders replaced your personal freedom and liberty with propaganda, advertisement, and entertainment that your own political leaders, religious leaders, and multinational corporations approved for the public or chose for the masses or wanted you to know so that they can limit your vision about the big picture of a free society somewhere else around the world, manipulating you for their own political, religious, and selfish agenda. So, my friends, where you are now is not the end of the world. It's just a part of it. So move out from your comfort zone, and embrace the coming republic of the whole world.

From Persians to Babylonians to Greeks to Romans to all the fallen empires, one thing that is historically sure in this world we live in is that evil has much power. Forget the preacher that told you Jesus has defeated the devil.

No evil still has power here in this world, but one thing again that is sure is a proof that good has much power, which gratifies minds of people of peace that long live the globe of freedom and liberty, for we will get there very soon.

History has often been written not by victors, kings, leaders, and rulers but by the vanquished or at least those who tell their own story from the vantage of their aggrieved, pained, and often enslaved forbearers. Examples are slavery and the Holocaust. That fact should not suggest to our generation that all past empires were led by bad kings.

The genocide of six million Jews by the Nazis under Hitler was evil. The slaves sold from Africa to the New World was evil. In 1994, just three years after American and Russian leaders signed the first Strategic Arms Reduction Treaty (START I).

The international community failed to provide a coherent response to the genocide in Rwanda. The nature and scale of this genocide have prompted substantial study and analysis, along with deep soul-searching among policy makers and observers. In an attempt to eliminate Rwanda's Tutsi minority, the Hutu majority systematically slaughtered eight hundred thousand individuals, most of them civilians, in just one hundred days, a rate of killing that rivals the worst in human history. Armed with machetes, the killers were both vicious and organized, torturing their victims, murdering them in cold blood, and dumping their bodies in mass graves. In numerous cases, such killings took place while international peacekeepers stood by helplessly. The Rwandan genocide exposed glaring weaknesses in the capacity of international and multilateral institutions to prevent or respond to such violence while raising troubling questions about international willingness to do so. But good rose up under the arm of other leaders to put an end to the dehumanization of the Jews and African Americans. This fact of history should not be an excuse for the Jews or Americans' suspicion of the new world order that is in the making.

This is the first time in six thousand years that people have carried out a revolution against a pharaoh in Egypt. What will follow the events in North Africa and the Middle East is the emergence of a new world order followed by the coming into place of a *one-world government*.

There are good leaders with good intentions and ideas, love of God, and love of their own people who will carry this assignment out.

Term Limits for Political Officeholders around the World

We are in crucial days in world history, and this is preeminently the right time to speak the truth, the whole truth, boldly and forcefully, making fear become afraid in this global village.

My long ambition from childhood was that when I grow up was focused toward working out plans to make people happy instead of making them miserable. There is a juncture in life where you must choose between two roads, and where you end up is the choice you made at the junction of decision. I am proud to inform the world that I have chosen to be on the side of the truth and shun every opportunity to be counted among those who abuse economic and political power for self-gratification and those who believe that it is their birthright or color of their skin or length of their nose to rule the world and that if they can no longer rule the world, they have to ruin the world.

Those in the Middle East who are currently struggling to democratize their systems of governance would do well to take a hard look at the US model, not just to copy its positive aspects—and there are many—but to avoid its palpable weaknesses.

42

The new democrats of the Arab Middle East doubtlessly feel that they have more fundamental concerns at present in trying to win and sustain their fundamental political rights. Painful history has certainly taught them the need for term limits for presidents and other executives. But if they are wise, they will heed the negative model of the US Congress and ensure that those they elect to newly empowered legislatures reside within a system that aligns the motives of the legislators with those of the people whom they serve. If the newly democratized wish to control their destinies over the long term, they need to ensure that their representatives are not only elected by them but also are truly of them. The current US legislative system did not spring forth from the minds of the US founding fathers intact and immutable. Like any system, it evolved over time.

What was the intent of the framers of the US Constitution? Their vision was one of citizen legislators who would temporarily put aside their careers in business, their professions, or academia to serve the public for a time before returning to their communities. Those who originally conceived the US system did not foresee the rise of a permanent class of professional legislators motivated to ignore the greater good in order to sustain themselves in office.

Polls show conclusively that Americans are greatly concerned with the national debt, even if they disagree strongly about how to cut it. The same polls, unsurprisingly, show popular disdain for a congress whose political cowardice and fecklessness were so prominently on display during the recent crisis over the US debt ceiling.

Citizens' disdain, however, usually does not extend to their own congressmen. Why? Because in the desperate effort to win federal dollars, an individual congressman's worth is determined not by her ability to change a dysfunctional system, which she can hardly do alone, but by ensuring a fair share for her constituents. Remember, in Washington, congressmen are not citizen-legislators, but professionals. Their influence, measured by their ability to get money for their states and districts, is not determined by merit but by seniority.

A voter who might otherwise be tempted to send a message to Washington and try to change the wasteful and self-serving culture of the Capitol knows that the result of voting his or her congressman out of office will most likely be to gratuitously disadvantage one's own locality in the zero-sum competition for federal money.

Term limits for elected politicians everywhere on this planet are needed in a new world order.

From Franklin Roosevelt to Bill Clinton and even the way Bush invaded Iraq, it is no secret that US leadership for over a century has secretly made global governance an American project; while this was going on in the White House and US congressional chambers, ordinary United States citizens were made to have the view that the idea of a one-world government is an unnatural act that is against the Christian principles of our founding fathers who are using Judeo-Christian media propaganda to attack the idea of a one-world government. On radio, television, and preaching on church pulpits, American preachers' sermons focus best on connecting biblical prophecies of evil to make the public believe that the idea of a one-world government is satanic; but behind the scene, it remains an American project that will never be on the ballot until it comes into full.

We already know that the case of Bush's Iraq War resulted in a backlash that blew the lid open that a new world order is now in the making.

The Islamic clerics, on the other hand, are being used to propagate fear around the idea of a one-world government, which is one of the reasons that made Iran view the emergence of a new world order as a threat to Islam, which is one of the reasons Iran has chosen to sponsor Hamas, Hezbollah, and Assad of Syria in defiance of people's quest for democracy in the Middle East as being witnessed by the Arab revolution. The Arab spring objective is not to protect the religion of Islam. It is basically an aspiration of Arab people for a peaceful society, freedom, justice, liberty, and equal economic and political opportunities in their own nations. Today the events around the world have demonstrated one truth: that the only superpower in the Middle East is the united Arab people's opinion, and this united Arab people's opinion is more powerful than the government of the United States and Iran in that region. The united people's opinion is the only superpower that will subdue Iran as a sponsor of state terrorism against world peace in the Middle East.

Americans like to think of themselves and their country as a model for the world. Indeed, this attitude of self-congratulation is one of the least attractive aspects of US culture when viewed from abroad. Even Americans themselves are barely aware of it. For most Americans, this common faith in the superiority of many aspects of their society—from popular entertainment, to higher education, to the judicial system, and so on—is part of the web of shared assumptions that underlie US culture. And among these, nothing is so firmly fixed in the American mind than the inherent superiority of their democratic political system.

The world has been treated to the spectacle of the vaunted two-party American political system as it has driven the government heedlessly to the very brink of a disastrous default on its debt payments. This national financial near miss and the profound skepticism it has generated concerning the United States' long-term ability to put its fiscal house in order have roiled global stock markets and threaten, if not soon addressed, to upend the dollar-based global financial system that has been in place since the end of World War II. Whether such a change in the global financial system is a good or bad thing over the long term, I cannot say, but it would not happen without severe global economic dislocations, from which all would suffer.

On the surface, it would appear that the dysfunction at the heart of the US Congress is due to the ideological inflexibility of both Democrats and Republicans in making self-interested appeals to their respective constituencies. The former refuse necessary cuts in social benefits, while the latter refuse to contemplate even sensible tax increases. Together, they reflect an apparent refusal on the part of Americans to live within their means. Indeed, that refusal—reflected in huge, endemic, and unsustainable trade and budget deficits and in the rapidly accelerating growth of the US national debt—is abetted by the dollar's status as a reserve currency, which has greatly moderated what for any other nation and any other currency would be enormous downward pressure on exchange rates. Thus, the world's faith in the United States has served to reward American faithlessness.

Particularly, as they have been shielded from some of the worst immediate effects of their profligacy, Americans' lack of fiscal discipline should come as no surprise. It would be hard, however, to make the case that their irresponsibility is owing to something unique in the US national character.

To understand the core of the problem in the US system, one must look deeper—at the nature of the system itself.

In the meantime, to the extent that world prosperity is placed at risk by the irresponsibility of the US Congress, all should hope that Americans will be stirred by the current crisis to address one of the manifest shortcomings of their own political culture.

God is not interested in ruling a man without his consent. When he gave the Ten Commandments to Israel, he told Moses to read it to them, and Moses shed a blood of sacrifice. And the Israelites responded that "We agree with you, Jehovah," so Moses sprinkled the blood on the people as a covenant that "We are one on these rules, not that God wants to police our lives, but we agree together that this is how best we need to live together as fathers to his children in this covenant." The rest of the world is sick and tired of American projects of secret global governance from the White House, Pentagon, Congress, or State Department without the consent of other nations in the union of this planet, so the time has come for all of us to come together under the banner of brotherhood and sisterhood and agree together on how we move forward with a new world order.

The United Nations and NATO resolution on Libya; the revolution in Egypt, Tunisia, Syria, Yemen; and the Israel-Palestine conflict may end up letting the world accept the fact that the United States remains the last empire to bow down for the one-world government in the making since there are only two superpowers in our world today: the United States and public opinion. And this position is the global governance that was cleverly put into place as a secret American project. It is the same position that Israel wants in the Middle East, with the support of the United States, using the issue of Palestine as a stepping stone to realize a dominant superpower unchallenged in the Middle East but it will not happen, giving consideration to the Arab League, who may want to demand Palestine as the 194th member of the United Nations, with East Jerusalem as its capital. Whatever this leads to is part of the new world order in the making.

President Harry Truman of the United States came up with his own doctrine of protecting other nations in the name of stopping the spread of communism. Does that one stop the Soviet Union from exploding nuclear weapons, or does Truman stop communists from taking over China? Do Americans stop the Koran from breaking out? The collapse of the Soviet Union in 1991 that ended the Cold War, was it because of the United States' magic of policemanship of the world? Was it President Bush's invasion of Iraq, spending $3 trillion of American taxpayers' money, that started the North African and Middle Eastern revolution in Tunisia and Egypt? It was started by the action of one man. I mean what one hundred thousand soldiers that died in Bush's Iraq War failed to accomplish was done in Egypt by Egyptians themselves in eighteen days. Will Iran become the baby that troubled the Arab waters? What any US president worries most about is the rise of radical, fundamentalist Muslims having access to biological or chemical or nuclear capabilities. Every US president fears it and makes it a political agenda of Washington to instill it on all of us Americans, who must be frightened of Middle Eastern people too, just like the people who reside in the White House. Do we continue to run our world based on Washington's fear and mistrust of other nations' faith and culture?

I believe what the machine gun has failed to do in our world can be achieved through a new world order of respect to other people's liberty within the parameter of their own culture and belief system in their own backyard.

Muslims can govern themselves. The rest of the world should help them realize the blessing of freedom and liberty, which they have now initiated themselves. Let the West help them become a society free from the grip of religious fanaticism. Liberty is transformative. Give the Muslims hope that they will be welcomed as a free society that marginalizes the extremists. We cannot be going to other nations from the West like we do now in Iraq and Afghanistan on the excuse of protecting or safeguarding our own people. The next agenda should now be to help make North Africa and the Middle East a free society; then the extremists will wither away among them over time. Their own people will turn against the evil in their midst. That was how the war in Iraq was won, not by America's superpowered military machine guns, but by the use of concerned Iraqi citizens to fight it out with the extremists among them. Provide support and recognition to the revolutionaries' youths and technocrats among them who are not religious fanatics, and let them win the battle against the fundamentalists themselves. Freedom is not free. If you want it in your own country, fight for it, or remain slaves forever under the multinational corporations that are now more powerful than the political leaders of your country.

The United States does not want Iran to become a dominant regional player in the Middle East because that will mean a challenge to the United States' interest—a reason the United States does not want Iran to use negotiations as a cover-up while they continue to improve their nuclear capability. So the problem of the Middle East is simply a tug-of-war between Iran and the United States, not between Israel and Palestine, not between Christianity and Islam. It is a political war between the United States and Iran because the United States does not want other great superpowers in the Middle East, which is what Iran would like to be. So the United States is causing problems in the Middle East, supporting autocratic leaders like Saudi Arabia with their rules and state laws against women driving in Saudi Arabia—while the numbers of women drivers in Los Angeles outnumber men drivers, while nearly all MTA bus drivers are women and 65 percent of women in America are now sick and tired of having a husband but want free sex and children out of marriage. We are supporting leaders of other nations who oppress women and keep four at a time inside one house, women who cover their face when they go out for shopping. Does the United States love freedom for the women in the gulf, or are our political leaders just there to protect their own business investments on military weapons; export of troops' food, drinks, and uniforms to marine posts; and import of crude oil back home?

The United States is not concerned about ordinary, poor, oppressed folks of the gulf states under the kind of primitive rulers put in place over there by Washington Apache group and Londoner Club, but the cohesion of American allies in the Middle East is to stop the game of Iranians, Hezbollah, and Hamas with Syria shifting sides. It's time for the United States to get out of the Middle East and concentrate paying its debt of trillions of dollars back to China and Japan. Concentrate on marital economic revolution going on here at home, where women have taken over every home as both father and mother. Bring our troops home. Let there be a Palestinian state side by side, living in peace with Israel as neighbors, or make Israel the fifty-first state like Puerto Rico under the coming North American Union. Let the US Congress pass a law that allows allocation of plots of lands to the Jews from the area of lands we took from the Indians and the Mexicans if the new border makes Israel too small a land to occupy. At least God did not allocate to them Beverly Hills in Los Angeles. They got it from us and kept us back in Compton and Crenshaw and gave West Los Angeles to Chinese immigrants who came to America with 30 percent down payment the US citizens never had. The Bank of America took houses from African Americans, made them homeless, and sold the property to Chinese immigrants who came to the country with 30 percent down payment and a good FICO score.

So why is it that what happens here to us that we keep quiet and accepted is not acceptable to the Jews in Israel? Let us end these games of wars around the world. The Bible preachers say that when Jesus comes back in his glory, he will descend on Mount of Olives. That day he will take back the land from the Arabs and give it back to the Israelites, his chosen people, according to Pastor John Hagee. Jesus is coming back very soon. If you believe that, then let's reserve the rest of the Middle Eastern war for Jesus's return and his angels, and let us use our taxpayers' money for Medicare, Social Security, health-care delivery services, education, food, security, and education of our people. Stop ruling us with fear and Washington's military hegemony in the Middle East falsely based on the fear that if they came with a plane on September 11, 2001, they are planning to come back next September with biological weapons.

It seems to me that Israel's system of justice has not changed in the past two thousand years. Consider the book of Matthew chapter 5: when Jesus healed a man who had been sick, paralyzed, and handicapped for thirty-eight years, what did the Jews say? They accused Jesus of doing the healing and deliverance of a man from a thirty-eight-year-old problem on a Saturday, because Moses's Ten Commandments two thousand years earlier was against doing good on public holidays. And today the conflict on the Palestine state is simply traced back to the same old argument that God gave the Jews that portion of land about four thousand years ago, and they want it back now. When will the US Congress give California back to Mexico? Why fence out these people from their own homes and make them refugees across the border? "Netanyahu, tear down this wall" and accept negotiations for peace. Church leaders supported this kind of wall fencing? And if you don't agree with these church leaders, you are seen as the anti-Christ in their prayer meetings. And when you fail to fall down and die and you show up again at another Wednesday prayer meeting or Sunday service, the preacher, leaders, deacons, and ushers get surprised that God did not answer their prayer to kill you because you are against Israel. "Why is this black Nazi still alive?" And you are in trouble if your car is repossessed or you fall into foreclosure, then preachers will give testimony from their bully pulpits of how you have been cursed by God for going against Israel, not paying your tax, third sins, your refinance your mortgage and you and your wife kept part of it from Apostle Peter. "Fall down and die. In Jesus's name, amen." But thank God Almighty, I am still here with no high blood pressure. And if you are a Los Angeles resident in the USA, all they will do to you in Los Angeles superior court is a gang of Jewish attorneys and commissioners and justices at the city attorney Masonic temple to mess up your case on the court hearing date with the instructions to the judge on the bench. You lose if your money can only go far enough to hire a black attorney to represent your case. A black man with a black attorney as defendant before a white judge Dodson, facing a white Jewish lawyer? What do you get other than a Jewish verdict? What kind of New Testament Bible are you reading from, you Zionist preachers? Causing problems in our world, distributing the spirit of fear and superstitions to your congregation and the world through your television programs here and there about praying for the Jews and Israel, and that the American judicial system should be employed as a weapon to punish those who have opposing views and ideas besides your own opinions hidden behind the false teaching of the Bible.

Military hegemony has become a necessary evil just like Guantánamo, which a black president does not have the power to shut down due to fear of the white power. Wars and wars around the world have now become a private business to give jobs to the retired boys and military contractors using American troops and police posts in all regions of the world. It is not just about protecting us but also about protecting someone's family business and military trade. Please, give me a break. Let freedom reign in our new world. I am not Netanyahu, the prime minister of Israel. I am just an Abednego who came here to America by airplane, not by boat, because Nigerian chiefs never engaged in selling their kids as slaves to the New World. When they tried it in my village, they failed. My great-grandfather said they would rub okra on their hands. You try to catch them as slaves with okra on their hands, and Nigerians will slip away from slave traders. I may not have money like you, but I came from a smart family who was smart enough to use okra to escape slavery. Okra saved my fathers from slave masters. That is why I came here to the United States by aircraft, not by boat, so I do not have opportunity of a Hawaiian birth certificate behind my business card. The only thing people like us do is purchase a Roman citizenship like Paul's father; and I know that if I was born about three thousand years ago, they probably would arrest me for my books and put me in a fiery furnace of fire just like Shadrach, Meshach, and Abednego. And if I was born two thousand years ago, during the reign of Tiberius Caesar, the Jewish leaders would have used this message and my statements here now in support of some Bible teachers in my own church to cut off my head like John the Baptist instead of cutting off my bank account as a reformist preacher like Herod's wife did to John the Baptist or like temple leaders and teachers of laws did to Jesus Christ for disrupting the peace of the community and not staying out of the politics of the Pharisees and Hippocratic attorneys and judges at their Hill Superior Courts of that day. The court clerks and commissioners who were the Jewish sect that promoted strict interpretation of Mosaic laws and Judeo-Christianity. But thank God Almighty I am in the United States in 2011, *standing before you*, giving this speech.

I never wanted to acquire material possession in order to be rich and famous or live in a big mansion on a beachfront or live in a ranch. To me, riches are not only about money because there are some things money cannot buy. I want to help to put a stop to malaria, HIV/AIDS, and the widespread abject poverty in our world. If you look around today, there is a lack of computers, obesity, and access to nutritious food and good drinking water—unless you have money to buy drinking water from water manufacturers and pay extra tax to the government for the purchase of water to drink so both government and private enterprises now are selling water, which God gave to man for free like oxygen to live anyway. Oxygen is also for sale at emergency hospitals and clinics.

I want to help put a stop to heart diseases and female teenagers having children because they need a man or must marry a man to survive in our world. I want to help female refugees and illegal immigrants dispersed around the world for prostitution to survive, waiting twenty-eight years as women immigrants for a green card that will never be approved until Jesus Christ comes. And despite my good intention, it is rather unfortunate for me that I was not born into a wealthy family, which is the main reason I became a victim of capitalism and religion, praying for money in church that a miracle will make money rain down from heaven on me for years—until I became a member of AARP and realized that if you need money, you got to work for it, pastor, or get it by invoking Malachi 3:10.

I wasted my youthful and energetic life praying in the churches instead of playing the game in a capitalist society to get rich financially; and the world got to a stage that as a man, if you don't have money or a job, you cannot get a wife except baby mamas or part-time concubines who will call you only when they need to use you for the moment as a man. Anyway, that is another story you can read from my published books. The only chance left for me in my life is to speak truth to power without compromising the facts out of fear. Radically, I have publicly identified myself with the focus and objective to be part of something that is trying to benefit the majority of the world population as opposed to being part of something that is trying to identify with the folks who have already made it and refused to accept that our loving God made one man inferior to the other because of height, color of skin, or the length of a man's nose.

The fact that my nose is flat does not mean I inhale lesser oxygen than you with your longer, more pointed nose. All men are created equal and loved equally by God, for God so loved the world that he gave his only son to this world that whoever believes in him shall not die but have everlasting life. He did not send his son to the world to condemn the world, but that through him, the world might be saved and justified. The new testament with man by Almighty only one God is far more superior than Abraham's covenant and the Jewish covenant as recorded in the Torah under the Mosaic law. This is a new covenant that God established with all mankind—Jews, Arabs, Africans, Asians, Americans, all men and women on earth, with no respect or regard to a man's color of skin, geographical location, or the shape of a man's nose.

Pastor Hagee has told us that the Catholic church is the great whore and an apostate church, and he so strongly believes and expects that Jesus will come to defend Israel in Armageddon and toss into a fiery pit Iran, Russia, and all the Arab states for fighting against Israel. Why can't we just delay these wars in our world a little bit further until Jesus comes back? What about that preacher who said Jesus will come on May 21, 2011, which made me stop payment of my bills in hope that my debts will be canceled from May 22, 2011 by the coming back of Jesus Christ? Now their prophecy made me get behind in my mortgage, car notes, phone bills, and all my other bills to my corporate masters. Well, let's believe Pastor Hagee and the prophets, and let us use our time to make this world better and create a peaceful coexistence of living together with one another in a comity of nations and leave this matter like Pastor Hagee has said, waiting for God, who created this problem in the first place with his friend Abraham, a polygamist with many children from different baby mamas, which the Bible interpreted then as concubines.

EMMANUEL ADETULA

God chose Isaac, one of PA Abraham's children. The rest of the children he dispersed into the oil-rich gulf. He sent my great-grandmother's kids to Africa, same from Abraham. Remember, one of the grandchildren of Noah is named Egypt and founded Egypt, so God is the one that we need to wait for to come back and solve the problem he created in his own way. And let us, mankind, in our generations begin to work toward a new world of religious peace and order before the coming of John Hagee's Armageddon, when all the Catholics and the pope with the Iranian people will be thrown into the pit of hell by the coming back of Jesus in his fight between his holy angels and Ahmadinejad's coming seven imams—the Mahdis. Christians are expecting Jesus while Muslims are expecting the Mahdis to fight among themselves in a world wrestling match televised on the sky, where the whole world will be watching the events live on a supernatural bowl day, which will be an end to this matter. For now our concerns as citizens of the world should be having a world of peace, liberty, social justice; eradicating poverty, hunger, and disease; and stopping the privatization of drinking water by multinational corporations. This is very important to mankind now, more than the argument about interfaithism and Christ Islamism.

The assignment given to me as a Christian is to pray for the peace of Jerusalem, love the peace of Jerusalem, and work toward peace within the walls that will stand to establish peace and statehood of Israel and Palestine toward a new world order of peace. Then prosperity will come to our world. It is when the United Nations will come up with a bold declaration, action, and support for a peaceful wall between the two, making Palestine the 194th member of the United Nations.

Let's Jaw Jaw and let us wait the War War for the coming messiahs of Islam and the Lord Jesus Christ of Christianity in that jaw jaw now remains the only organized hope of man in the new world order, not war war. God bless Republican Tutius Orbis.

The Ombudsman of A New World Order

Cursing and Blessing of Israel

Anti-Semitism and the Kennedy Family Curse

In the fourth century, the church began to trade the authority of Christ for the authority of the emperor of Rome, and they began to trade the power of the Holy Spirit for the power of the army that kept the peace of Rome, and the world began to become confused over the nature of authority of the church. We began to put people under people who were to have authority over them and called it the authority of church, which has now brought the church leaders to misinterpretation of the Bible to trade the power of Christianity to keep the power of the state of Israel, just as it was used to keep the peace of Roman occupation of other people's lands. It is this confusion that we need to correct in the new world order that is in the making.

We are to take back the authority of Jesus not to bind and coerce but to set people free to obey his will and walk in the kingdom of our God with no bias to the Jews or Gentiles, Christians or Muslims, because Jesus died for the whole world.

In the State of Palestine, the mayors of Ramallah, Birzeit, Bethlehem, Zababdeh, Nazareth, Jifna, Ein 'Arik, Aboud, Taybeh, Beit Jala and Beit Sahour are Christians. The governor of Tubas Marwan Tubassi is a Christian. Suha Arafat, the widow of

Palestinian president Yasser Arafat and former first lady, is a Christian. The former Palestinian representative to the United States Afif Saffieh is a Christian, as is the ambassador of the Palestine in France Hind Khoury.

The Palestinian women's soccer team has a majority of Muslim girls, but the captain, Honey Thaljieh, is a Christian from Bethlehem. Many of the Palestinian officials such as ministers, advisers, ambassadors, consulates, and heads of missions, PLC, PNA, PLO, Fatah leaders, and others are Christians. Some Christians were part of the affluent segments of Palestinian society that left the country during the 1948 Arab-Israeli War by Israel.

In West Jerusalem, over 51 percent of Christian Palestinians lost their homes to the Israelis. I say this for you to know that the problem between Israel and Palestine is not a religious matter between Christians and Muslims. The problem between Palestine and Israel is one of the most powerful driving forces behind the "God and country" mentality. *Freemasonry*, founded by the US government in 1776, in reality, is a humanist institution that has formed the philosophy of statehood of Israel and America today in the name of patriotism, the love of one's country, which entered the Christian church with the principle of misinterpreting the Bible for mass political support of government actions in both Israel and the United States. The Gospel, which was given for salvation of the soul of man, has now become a tool in the hands of Zionist preachers in America to create support for political actions groups. Freemasonry's vulnerability to every form of corruption and abuse is what made them seek some Western preachers to use Christianity to force all Christians into supporting the state of Israel against the desired peace of Israel and its Arab neighbors.

My arguments are plain and unlearned except in the school of sound common sense under the influence of Christian principles. My ideas have a force that the learning of rabbis and talent of religious preachers of this world cannot gainsay or resist. I have truth on my side; though my statements, actions, and writings are dressed in a humble garb, they are mightier than error though clothed with the brilliancy of imagination, the pomp of declamation, and the cunning of sophistry. God hath chosen me, Emmanuel Adetula, the weak thing of this world, who cannot boast of my birth and pedigree or of my ancient and illustrious family, who has no titles of honor to aggrandize myself nor estates, possessions, good accent of speech that is sweet of hearing to the Western media.

I have no worldly substance to support myself with. Nevertheless, by the deliberate and free action of God's graciousness, I will confound the things that are mighty in this planet. In Shemoth Rabba, sec. 17, fol. 117, it is said, "There are certain matters which appear little to men, yet by them God points out important precepts." Instead, God chose things the world considers foolish in order to shame those who think they are wise. Paul the rabbi made this quote in Shemoth Rabba to his letters to Christians at Corinth in Corinthians 1:27, which says that God chose things that are powerless to shame those who are powerful. I have been chosen for a time like this in this history of man.

God gave me the word: blessed is the man or woman that helps me to publish it.

The rise of Hitler and his assault on Britain around 1940 were the events that led to the so-called *Kennedy family curse* in the USA. Joe Kennedy, as the then US ambassador to Britain, badly misjudged God and the Nazis' intentions though Kennedy was a Christian Catholic. Joe became a vocal critic of those who saw Hitler as an enemy of the Jewish people because Joe Kennedy said that the Jewish people deserved such threats to their existence from Nazis because Jews are bad people, but the truth is that God has chosen this bad people of this planet called the Jews by his own grace and favor, and such grace was not based on the Jews' morality.

God's favor was not based on the Jews' good attitude, character, or disposition. Since Joe Kennedy did not understand God's ways of choice, Joe Kennedy was unsympathetic to the plight of the Jews in 1940 and therefore concluded politically and commonsensically that the Jews brought the plight they faced with Nazis on themselves by their own actions, which is true socially, politically, and economically, but spiritually, that is not God's ways of doing things. God's methods are foolishness to man's ways. His ways make no conventional sense in politics, and because Joe Kennedy did not support the Jews in their plight with the Nazis as the US ambassador to Europe, he cut for himself and his children what Americans referred to as the Kennedy family curse.

After he lost his own ultimate ambition to become *President Joe Kennedy* of the United States, even his son that became president of the United States later was shot by assassination bullets. This is one of the mythologies of love and hate of the Jewish people in our world. Today Zionist preachers like Pastor continue to capitalize upon this myth to fabricate a fearful, spiritual phenomenon to scare Christians and the American people into forced support of the state of Israel, whether they are right or wrong, in respect to the Arab and Israeli conflict in the Middle East. In regard to Israel as a chosen people of God, there is an old proverb that says, if you are going in the village route and meet on the way a Jew and a snake, trust the snake and kill the Jew because a Jew is worse than a poisonous snake.

You will not believe this until you do business with a Jew, and this is the kind of people that God has chosen as his own people. It is therefore for me to conclude that the root cause of this world's problems emanated from God the creator himself. His principle of favor, grace, and choosing process of one man over another, one nation over another, loving one and hating another are not fair. God's favor is not fair. It is not always based on might or power, not by how good you are, not on morality, but by his grace and his favor and his mercy. This is beyond human commonsensical judgment. That is why today, we have problems in our world. Why should God choose the Jews, who are less than 1 percent of the world population, in his own infinite favor over the rest, the 99 percent—six billion of us?

Why did he have to choose Isaac, the father of Israel, over Ishmael, the father of Iran? Why did he love the Jews so much over the Arabs, their neighbors?

The mystery of God baffles you most when you consider why God chose me, Emmanuel Adetula, as the ombudsman of a new world order. He positioned me here in the United States for this assignment to be the chief protagonist of a new world order despite the fact that I cannot boast of my birth and pedigree, of my ancient and illustrious family, that I have no titles of honor to aggrandize me, but God chose me anyway because he best judges what men are in their heart and what measures serve the purposes of his glory. I may look like a fool to you right now, but I have been chosen by God for a time like this.

So the problem of this world is simply about the fact that mankind is in conflict and disagreement about God's ways of doing things in the kingdom of man, and every generation fights to get God out of world control and management of this planet. The world's desire is to chase God out of human lives because his ways are not our ways. His thoughts are never our thoughts. God never grew up learning democratic values and supporting the idea of Western democracy, that the majority must have their ways and the minority have their say with street protests and roam the streets with banners and placards before police armored vehicles or go and form an unregistered political tea party that, at the end of the day, will still end up a minority just like when they were protesters on the streets.

God always thinks he knows better than all of us. He does things the way he wants, and he never considers our feelings and ambitions and interests at all. God thinks this world belongs to him, and therefore he treats us as mere tenants and caretakers and resident managers employees who are just here to manage his property and plantation farmland and what else he apportioned to each of us in a limited term of service, and no one knows when he will show up and say, "Today you got to go from mortality into mortality."

He terminates our existence from there and gives our position and possessions to others, and men pass away to the unknown, so wars and problems come from this simple fact that we, in our own ambition and wisdom, set goals and objectives based on our own agenda.

Our motives in pursuit of world glory, honor, and power; doing everything in our strength to get and keep more worldly possessions for ourselves and for our own family; struggling every day to control more gold, silver, oil, minerals, land; manufacturing war machines and guns to keep or defend what we have got—we kept ourselves busy day in and day out to get more, more, and more until one day our world got to the stage where we are today, where only six thousand individuals become the owners of this planet while they now make the rest of the six billion of this world population into workers, tenants, and debtors of their own international monetary family. Even nations with natural resources are now under the control of nations with military power. Few nations now live as parasites on the rest of the nations of the world. Great nations make citizens of weak nations as have-nots. Those who never had have become the haves while turning the haves to have-nots; and few haves continue to dominate and control the have-nots, maintaining the status quo until we have a world system that enslaves others in slave-to-master relationships, villain-and-victims relationships, oppressed and conquerors, winners and losers in the comity of nations, because God's system is to choose the weak thing over the strong or to despise things that are mighty but celebrate the weaker, judging by God's ways of managing this world system, which is in opposition to our own perceptions and values as human beings. This autocracy versus democracy is the root cause of the present world problems, because let's face the fact.

Why should the Bible preachers tell us that God loves Israel and the Jews, which constitute about 2 percent both in population and land, less than the 98 percent of Arabs in population and land? That does not make sense to the world, because this is one of the greatest problems of the Middle Eastern conflict today. Would the world embrace an autocratic judgment of God as regards the Jews or the democratic idea of democracy that is sweeping around the Arab world today in solving the Israel and Palestine problem? Or do we continue to believe that God is right and any democratic idea of "let the majority rule," which has been the legacy of the Kennedy family, be swept under the carpet? This is the bedrock of resolution that must be considered a solution to the Arab-Israel conflict.

There is an ugly rumor that claims that grace takes us out of the jurisdiction of the law so that we do not have to obey the law. But Rabbi Paul, in his letter to Christians at Rome, wrote, *May It Never Be!* "For sin shall not be master over you, for you are not under law but under grace. What then? Shall we sin because we are not under law but under grace? May it never be!" (Rom. 6:14–15). This same twisted logic claims that when Christ came to fulfill the law, he kept the law for us so that we do not have to keep it. However, Christ says that he came to establish the law, which shall abide forever: *The Eternal Nature of the Law.* "Do not think that I came to abolish the Law or the Prophets; I did not come to abolish but to fulfill. For truly I say to you, until heaven and earth pass away, not the smallest letter or stroke shall pass from the Law until all is accomplished" (Matt. 5:17–18).

Jesus did not save us from the wages of sin so that we can continue to sin. Neither did Christ demonstrate the eternal nature of the law so that we can abandon it with scorn for eternity. Christ came to demonstrate the fact that under certain conditions, the descendants of Adam and Eve can keep the law and become good citizens of a larger society of the perfect, law-abiding citizens of the universe. Grace is simply a stay of the death penalty so that God can demonstrate his claims and institute. His process of rehabilitation is called the plan of salvation. Did God support a world system where it is difficult for us to live among ourselves in peace without taking what belongs to another neighbor forcefully for ourselves, without taking away the rights of others, their freedom of expression and association, and territorial rights of existence in their motherland? What God gave them is needed by us so we have to displace them to get what we want for ourselves by force and through acts of crook and warfare, so the world race is simply fighting against God's ways of ruling in the kingdom of man. That is why we have wars and not peace in our world today.

As a student of geography, the best way to understand the map of the world is not to hang it on the wall of your classroom, but you have to place it flat on the floor, step over it, and know that though it is under your feet, it is also above your head, and far below under your feet lies an endless ocean of water that takes you unto an endless universe. That is why your teachers told you that the world is a round globe, because what goes around comes around. What affects them over there will soon affect you right here.

We walk on this planet flat on our feet due to the force of the center of gravity, but the planet earth is not flat. And the history of mankind testifies to this truth that there is a power superior to the power of kings and kingdoms, presidents and prime ministers, bishops and imams; and it is that power that rules in the kingdom of man. God made this planet of ours like a circle because there is no end or corner in a circle, so that if a man keeps running from God, God will continue to pursue him until he gets tired of running, because where you get tired in the race of life is your own end in this circular race of life. And that is why, if someone is pursuing you, you have to keep running, because as you get tired, he himself is getting tired. Whosoever first gets sick and tired loses the race because there is no end or corner in the circular race of life.

We are running a 360-degree race, not 180 degrees, my friend. If you stop at 180 degrees, it was because your parents have run the 360, or maybe your own enemy got tired before it pursued you to the 180 degrees where you are having your victory right now, so your race is not my race, but I will keep running until my own enemies get tired because I cannot run away from God, from doing this dangerous job of telling the truth. God gave me the word, and I will publish it.

But I heard the Bible say that the heavens and heavens belong to God and this world he has given to the children of men; therefore, the sacred trust of every national government is to maintain the welfare of its own citizens. The world system is divided into nations and territorial boundaries; it is therefore the duty of nationals to first consider the interest of its own citizens and prevent social and economic injustice and aggressive encroachment of the desire of the few upon the rights of the many, for surely the few must have rights, but such rights cannot be preserved at the expense of the majority's human rights, which is the beauty of democracy. This principle of human justice is what will push the United Nations to consider the rights of the Arabs' majority over

Israelites', who are in the minority in the Middle East, and if the likes of Pastor John Hagee disagree with me and if the Netanyahu congress party in Capitol at Washington refuses to clap their hands for my statements here, they have no choice but to wait until Jesus comes to fight and win the battle for Israel in the battle of Armageddon. But man will do what man will do and let God do what he will do. That is one important step toward the new world order.

The rulers and managers of God's gifts and natural resources to mankind in our planet have failed this generation through their own incompetence and selfishness. The tyrants are now being rejected by the hearts and minds of all men in all places, particularly in Africa and the Middle East. The revolutions going on now in some parts of the world are sure signs of the dawn of a new world order that will make this world never the same again. The debt crisis around the world, the Internet revolution due to the information age, and the possible weakness in the US dollar's value will be part of the factors that will tighten the hand of the United States to act as an empire with enough power to withstand the dawn of the coming one-world government; and like everybody says, the United States will not support a demand by the rest of the world for a change of course until it runs out of all the options on the table.

If we are the creators of moral codes, then what we have is the assertion that God needed Jesus to die because we have trouble following rules we create for ourselves. Not only does that not make much sense, but it doesn't look much like traditional Christianity anymore. Therefore, God's favor has nothing to do with man-created moral codes of who is good or bad in our own cultural or traditional sense. That is why he chooses people not based human-set rules and moral standards.

No Christian has any authority over another Christian, but a church has authority over every Christian, so when a church agrees on one principle and you go against it as a single, individual Christian, the church leader will invoke the authority of the church to punish you. That does not mean the bishop or the pastor is holier or more powerful than you spiritually. That is why they want you to make a commitment and take membership in their local church. Once you do, you automatically come under the spiritual authority of that local church. If you are holier or have a better relationship with God than the leader of the local church, you have put yourself under his spiritual authority, and he then has the right to exercise spiritual authority over you.

You can join his church with five cars and end up with public transportation with no money for a bus pass if you did something wrong and he cursed you. Likewise, he can bless you from homelessness to apartment ownership by using the church's authority. So it is just using the authority of the church, which has now become the mythology of "If you curse Israel, you will be cursed, and if you bless Israel, you will be blessed," and it works. Why? Because church leaders have agreed to it as a norm of the religious standard. Likewise are the tithes. They agreed on it and made it a church pillar. If you pay your tithes, you will be blessed, and it works. So you have to understand that church power is established in corporate agreement under the authority of its leader. Any single individual that goes against it automatically puts himself under a curse.

If you don't know this truth, you will be wondering why it works if God did not support the idea. No, God does not have to like or initiate it, but since it is agreed as part of church-embedded doctrines, rules, and regulations of the church, God is bound to answer to the judgment of any believer who violates the rules when a church leader invokes such authority coming from a church leader or a ministry leader you have submitted yourself to. So if a pastor says to you that you will lose your car, your job, your house same time tomorrow and it did happen the way he said it despite the fact that you are in right standing with God and you pray, fast, and live a holy life, why is it that his prayer to God can make your life bitter? Why? God did not answer his prayer. God just respected the authority vested in the head of a church or a ministry.

That is why, as a believer, you should not put yourself under a man or a woman of God who has no love to be a good shepherd, because when you offend him, he will destroy your life and go about boasting about it later as if he had a power greater than another—you, a Christian brother. No pastor is greater than another believer next door, but every pastor has greater authority than members of his church, and God respects church authority. Such a scenario does not mean your pastor is more powerful or holier or closer to God than you are; he only uses the authority that God has made available to anyone that occupies the position that he is occupying as a leader of your local church. It is the authority of the church that has been hijacked by Israel for God and patriotism that has made it a taboo for anyone in a Christian community to oppose Israel with the fear of "Whosoever curses Israel will be cursed, and whosoever blesses Israel will be blessed." This does not emanate from God, but it is for sure protected and exercised under the authority of believers, just like paying of tithes based on God's principles of "Whatever you bind here on earth, I will bind in heaven." Finally, what I am pointing out here is that your pastor is not more powerful than you, but he has the authority of the church over you to heal, to bless, or to curse.

ABOUT THE AUTHOR

Dr. Emmanuel Adetula is best known for telling the truth and is counted among the most dynamic religious and social commentators in the making of a new world order. A religious leader and social entrepreneur with a master of arts in divinity, a doctor of philosophy in social work, and a holder of postgraduate certificates in negotiation and conflict management from USIP in Washington, DC, Emmanuel Oluwole Adetula, with eight books to his credit, was born in Nigeria, West Africa, and has been residing in the United States as a legal permanent resident since 1999. He was director of the CCN House Community Development Agency in Los Angeles from 2002 to 2011 and was founding resident of CCN Center for Religious Peace and New World Order, an organization whose mission is to seek and pursue good world governments, religious peace, liberty, and social justice by using research, dialogue, conferences, workshops, books, documentary films, TV and radio programs, Internet and social media as well as print media to achieve its mission in world communities. The organization promotion of the rule of law, transitional justice, and democracy features interviews and dialogues with political and religious leaders; the result of these dialogues contributed immensely to Emmanuel Adetula's messages, speech, and sermons, which are recorded in book, DVD, and CD formats.

CCN Center for Religious Peace is a division of Christ Channel Network (CCN) Inc. It is a bona fide 501(c) (3) nonprofit organization in the United States founded in 2002 by Rev. Emmanuel Adetula. He is in tremendous demand as one of the most dynamic speakers of our time; he receives invitation to speak in churches, colleges, and business corporations around the world. A former director of Olomi Community Bank, Interplanetal Company Ltd., and Tulalum Nigeria Ltd. from 1989 to 1998, he holds a Nigerian honorary traditional chieftaincy title as the Atolase of Ola. He is also a fellow member of the Association of Business Executives; a licensed and ordained minister; licensed by trade as a realtor, tax professional, notary public, mediator, and dispute resolution consultant; and a Title II diplomat/consultant and a notary public commissioned by the Los Angeles County and the State of California, USA.

If you are the one that God is talking to in helping to support this mission, do so today with your financial contribution of any amount from $150 and you will receive the complete package of the book, DVD, and CD combo shipped to you free as a thank-you gift for making a donation that demonstrates your support to the ministry of Dr. Emmanuel Adetula and the Center for Religious Peace and New World Order. Mail your donation to PO Box 111589, Los Angeles, CA 90011, USA. Or visit our website to place your order for either the book or DVD or CD based on the cost of each item as advertised at www.emmanueltula.com.

EMMANUEL ADETULA

www.ingramcontent.com/pod-product-compliance
Lightning Source LLC
Chambersburg PA
CBHW070257290326
41930CB00041B/2633